Original title:
Illusion

Copyright © 2024 Swan Charm Publishing
All rights reserved.

Editor: Jessica Elisabeth Luik
Author: Aron Pilviste
ISBN HARDBACK: 978-9916-86-032-8
ISBN PAPERBACK: 978-9916-86-033-5

## Dappled Ephemera

In the morning's gentle light,
Through leaves a dance unfolds,
Shadows weave a fleeting sight,
A story nature holds.

Breezes whisper soft and low,
Secrets in the trees impart,
Moments fleeting as they go,
Painting dreams upon the heart.

Sunbeams pierce the shady veil,
Glancing through the canopy,
Patterns flicker, slowly pale,
Ephemeral, yet so free.

Birdsong lingers in the air,
Echoes of a sunshine day,
Dappled light with tender care,
Guides the wanderer's way.

Twilight brings a softer hue,
As the daylight fades to rest,
Memories of light pass through,
In our hearts, forever blessed.

**Astral Charades**

Stars perform their silent dance
In the sky's eternal expanse
Planets spin in cosmic themes
Chasing light in fleeting dreams

Nebulas blend their hues with grace
Galaxies weave through endless space
Mystery shrouds the night's facade
In celestial, astral charades

## **Glimmering Phantoms**

Whispers in the twilight mist
Reflecting light the moon has kissed
Shadows flit from tree to tree
Phantoms glimmer, wild and free

Memories stitched in silver thread
Echoes of those long since dead
In the night, they dance and weave
Stories told, but few believe

## **Daedalus' Maze**

Winds whisper through ancient stone
Labyrinths where lost dreams have grown
Walls that twist with tales of old
In Daedalus' maze, secrets unfold

Paths that wind through timeless woe
Footsteps tread where none may go
Echoes of distant cries amaze
Lost forever in the maze

## **Nebulous Shadows**

In the void where shadows creep
Nebulas in darkness sleep
Wisps of light in shadows play
Nebulous forms till break of day

Mists and auras gently blend
Illusions round each cosmic bend
Shadowed paths where dreams confound
In nebulous realms, no light is found

## Ephemeral Brilliance

Fleeting as the morning dew,
Moments gilded, then retreats.
Sunrise paints the skies anew,
Ephemeral, brilliance fleets.

Glimpses of a starry night,
Lasting but a heartbeat's sound.
Light that carries pure delight,
Yet fades when dawn is found.

Seconds seize to paint the day,
Petals of a blooming rose.
In the swiftest, softest way,
Brilliance comes and quickly goes.

## **Glimmering Apart**

Sparkles in the distant night,
Twinkling lights that softly part.
Silent whispers of their plight,
Glimmers pulled from heart to heart.

Stars aligned in solo play,
Each its own celestial art.
Though they shine, they're far away,
In the heavens, glimmering apart.

Cosmic dance that never meets,
Waltzing in the void so vast.
Lonely glows that time defeats,
Bound by ancient stories cast.

## Traces of Vapors

Wisps that curl in morning air,
Ghostly trails that fade to none.
Lingering as though despair,
Touched by fingers of the sun.

Mystic paths that drift and fade,
Evanescent, soft as dreams.
Traces marked by twilight's shade,
Vapors caught in gentle streams.

Memory's faint silhouette,
In the ether, fleeting still.
Moments gone yet not forget,
Like vapors, their essence spill.

## **Wraithlike Dreams**

In the silent, moonlit hours,
Dreams arise like spectral forms.
Wraithlike in their fleeting powers,
Whisper soft through twilight's storms.

Visions veiled in misty lines,
Ephemeral as night's embrace.
They drift past the sands of time,
Leaving but a ghostly trace.

Haunting whispers in the night,
Fading soon with morning's beams.
Wraithlike dreams take fragile flight,
Lost within their shadowed schemes.

## **Celestial Glamour**

Stars that shimmer, soft and faint
In the sky, their tales they paint
Twinkling secrets, ether-bound
Silent whispers, magic found

Moonlight dances on the sea
A waltz of light, serenity
Galaxies stretch out their arms
Heaven's quilt of endless charms

Planets spinning, cosmic grace
Infinite, in stellar space
Constellations mark the signs
Tracing paths in deft designs

Meteor, a fleeting spark
Cuts across the night's dark arc
In its glow, a glimpse we see
Of the universe's glee

## **Phantom Riddles**

Shadows flicker on the wall
Voices echo in the hall
Mystery in every breath
Whispers from the world of death

Cloaked in mist, the silent night
Hides the truth from mortal sight
In the dark, an unseen hand
Threads through time, a ghostly band

Riddles wrapped in phantom guise
Seek the answers, tantalize
Answers float just out of reach
Curse and bless, they silent teach

Spirits of the ancient past
Timeless, haunting, holding fast
Their enigmas, whispered low
Secrets no one else could know

## Spectral Fabrics

Woven webs of spectral light
Glowing in the hush of night
Threads of gossamer and shade
Mystic patterns subtly laid

In the fabric, specters shift
Through the veil, to realms they drift
Seamless, in their ghostly guise
Invisible to human eyes

Colors born of twilight's gleam
Softly shimmer, softly dream
Tapestries of faded hues
In their folds, the past accrues

Phantoms weave their silent thread
Binding life to realms of dead
In each weave, a tale is spun
Of the journey yet begun

**Passing Fantasies**

Fleeting dreams, like morning mist
Vanish with the sun's first kiss
Ephemeral, the realms of thought
Drift away when they are sought

In the silence of the mind
Fantasies we chance to find
Moments bright, yet swiftly pass
Like reflections in a glass

Each illusion, soft and bright
Fades away with coming light
Hopes and fears, they slip like sand
Through the fingers of the hand

In the heart, desires bloom
Faint as flowers' brief perfume
Passing fantasies, they fly
Caught 'twixt earth and open sky

## Ethereal Veils

Through veiled mists that softly rise,
A world unseen before my eyes,
Soft whispers of the morning dew,
In twilight realms of skyward blue.

Beneath the shroud of ancient trees,
Where time's embrace sets spirits free,
The dance of shadows in moon's light,
Unfolds the magic of the night.

The echoes of forgotten realms,
Where silence sings and peace overwhelms,
Guarded by the stars' serene glow,
In veils of dreams the heart does flow.

## Ghosts of Reality

In corridors of time, they dwell,
The stories only shadows tell,
Echoes of a life once bright,
Now faded in the ghostly night.

They whisper truths long left unsaid,
In realms where we fear to tread,
Haunting memories leave their trace,
In the void of time and space.

Yet in their mournful, silent cries,
Lies the essence of our ties,
To the moments of our past,
In the phantom's spell we're cast.

## **Shadows and Phantoms**

Beneath the moon's ethereal grace,
Lie shadows in a cold embrace,
Phantoms of a forgotten lore,
Dance where light and darkness war.

By night they rise, in silence mute,
Playing their invisible flute,
Weaving tales of days long gone,
Echoes of a ghostly dawn.

From the depths of time's abyss,
They share a long-forgotten kiss,
In shadows where the light refrains,
Lie phantoms bound by unseen chains.

# Woven Whispers

In the loom of time's deep stride,
Whispers weave where shadows hide,
Threads of fate in silence twined,
Binding heart to heart and mind.

Through the whispers, stories blend,
Tales of love that know no end,
Softly spoken, secrets told,
In the fabric of the old.

Gentle as the night's cool air,
Woven whispers everywhere,
In the quiet, hear them sing,
The delicate touch of unseen strings.

## **Haze of Secrets**

Whispers float on twilight's breeze,
Murmurs veiled in spectral leaves,
Moonlight's tendrils twist and weave,
Lost in shadows, none perceive.

Silent echoes, old and gray,
Guardians of night and day,
Ancient tales in silence lay,
Haze of secrets, fade away.

Eyes in darkness softly gleam,
Guarding truths as if a dream,
In the night, reflections beam,
Veiling secrets, pure and theme.

## **Silver Veils**

Draped in silver, night's embrace,
Stars are shining in their place,
Mystic veils through space they trace,
Moonlit whispers, gentle grace.

Waves of shadows, soft and deep,
In their folds, the secrets keep,
In the silver, dreams will creep,
Echoes in the silent sweep.

Veils so thin, and yet they hide,
Mysteries on the other side,
In the silver mists, they bide,
Through the night, in beauty glide.

## **Ribbons of Smoke**

Ribbons of smoke, thin and gray,
Rise and twirl, then drift away,
From the fire, they softly sway,
Fading dreams at break of day.

In the air, their paths entwine,
Mystic dances, they design,
Through the night, in lines so fine,
Whispers of another time.

Silent trails in twilight's cloak,
Shape and form as passions stoke,
Skyward bound, the dreams invoke,
Soft as thread, these ribbons of smoke.

## **Fractured Gleams**

Fractured gleams in crystal night,
Stars that shimmer, cold and bright,
Splintering through ebon height,
Fragments pierce the dark with light.

Mirrored shards in heaven's dome,
Scattered far, but not alone,
In their gleaming, secrets comb,
Silent watchers in night's home.

Through the dark, their whispers scream,
Light that breaks and then redeem,
In the void, soft patterns scheme,
Fragments blend to form a dream.

## **Phantom Threads**

Woven by ghostly hands,
In a tapestry unseen,
Lie the stories of yore,
In a twilight's serene.

Caught in time's embrace,
Threads of silver gleam,
Whispering secrets lost,
In the corridors of dream.

A dance of shadows faint,
With memories interlace,
Phantom threads reveal,
The echoes of grace.

Unraveling at dawn,
Yet mending with the night,
A silent, endless loom,
Crafting tales in light.

Invisible to touch,
But felt within the soul,
Phantom threads connect,
Making the spirit whole.

## Subtle Charades

In shadows they play,
With a delicate art,
Masked in illusions,
They capture the heart.

Soft whispers of joy,
Or tears left unwept,
The dance of the subtle,
Where mysteries are kept.

Eyes turned to the sky,
Clouds form their parade,
In whispers and sighs,
Enacting charades.

Truth hidden in jest,
And laughter ensnares,
The soul of the seeker,
In subtle affairs.

With each gentle move,
A new truth displayed,
In the enigmatic world,
Of subtle charades.

## Web of Deception

Glistening in moonlight,
A web deftly spun,
Threads of silver lies,
Catch the morning sun.

Entrapped in its weave,
The truth struggles to break,
But whispers of deceit,
Echo with each quake.

Silken strands of falsehood,
Glimmer in the night,
Entwining the unwary,
In their lustrous might.

Eyes search for freedom,
In the labyrinth's snare,
But the web clings tighter,
In its deceitful lair.

Alas, a sword of truth,
Can cut these threads of gray,
Freeing the spirit bound,
In deception's vast array.

## Veil of Clouds

Mornings draped in silk,
Clouds woven with care,
The sky dons its veil,
In an ethereal glare.

Mountains shrouded soft,
Peaks hidden in mist,
A world wrapped in dreams,
By the dawn's gentle kiss.

Whispers in the wind,
Echo through the vast,
Veil of clouds lift,
Revealing the past.

Sunlight pierces through,
Threads of gold and white,
Lifting the horizon,
To a heavenly height.

In the day's embrace,
Dreams are gently spun,
Behind the veil of clouds,
Wonders have begun.

## **Fading Vistas**

Golden hills in twilight's gleam,
Soft and silent are the streams.
Whispered winds in twilight's light,
Guide the way into the night.

Fade away, the colors blend,
Into shadows without end.
Memories in hues of grace,
Glimmer in a timeless space.

Stars alight on velvet skies,
Twinkling with a thousand eyes.
Silent, still, the world at rest,
Nature's calm, forever blessed.

## **Nectar of Fog**

Misty veils soft embrace,
In the dawn's early face.
Whispers hint of things unseen,
Laced with evening's quiet dream.

Dew kissed petals gently bend,
Waves of haze that never end.
Silent specters wrap the day,
Foggy dreams in silver grey.

Echoes of a distant thrum,
Nature's verse in soft hum.
Through the mist, a path unveils,
Guided by the fog-bound trails.

## **Smoky Realities**

Plumes arise in morning's glow,
Shadows cast, a fleeting show.
Mislaid truths in tendrils curl,
Whispers of the hidden world.

Through the haze, clear voices drift,
Murmurs slow as visions shift.
Clouds of grey obscure the light,
Veiling day, embracing night.

In the depth of smoky lies,
Truth concealed in dark disguise.
Yet, in glimpses, sparks of real,
Break through clouds that softly steal.

## Token of Dreams

In the night, sweet slumbers call,
Through the veil, dreams lightly fall.
Tokens bright from realms unseen,
Gifted in the night's serene.

Star-bound wishes take to flight,
Navigating through the night.
Echoes of the heart's true quest,
Finding solace, finding rest.

Whispers soft, like silken thread,
Weave through dreams inside the head.
Waking light or twilight gleam,
Each a token of the dream.

## The Fog of Moments

In the mist of morning's breath,
Whispers drift, escaping death.
Shadows long and faces fleet,
Time and space in silence meet.

Branches reach through silver haze,
Sunlight strays in softened rays.
Footsteps echo, no one cries,
Memory's waltz beneath the skies.

Ghostly echoes write the air,
Songs of peace, a lover's prayer.
In the fog where past does spin,
Present folds and dreams begin.

Through the veil, the world refracts,
Truths and lies in subtle acts.
Moments pass, a fleeting dance,
Caught between life's happenstance.

In the end the mist subsides,
Clarity like breaking tides.
What was lost and now is found,
In the fog—all things unbound.

## Hall of Mirrors

In corridors with gleaming walls,
Reflections dance in endless halls.
Faces shift and forms reshape,
Truth and myth begin to drape.

Crystal frames and silvered glass,
Echoes from an age gone past.
Lost within the shifting lines,
Endless search for hidden signs.

Every step a question posed,
Every glance an answer closed.
In the maze of mirrored sights,
Daywalks blend into nightlights.

Refractions twist, revealing more,
Answers weave through mirrored door.
Doubts dissolve in endless turn,
As shadows of the self discern.

Within this hall of mirrored panes,
Identity's reflection wanes.
Truth behind the glass appears,
Revealed in moments, hidden years.

## Chasing Shadows

Through the twilight dim and cool,
Figures glide as spirits rule.
Whispers weave in shadowed lore,
Footsteps echo evermore.

Beneath the moon's soft argent glow,
Shadows dance and secrets flow.
Every turn a fleeting game,
Chasing whispers without name.

In the forest deep and still,
Silent spectres bend to will.
Branches weave a shadow's path,
In their wake, a silent laugh.

From the dusk to breaking dawn,
Shapes persist in light withdrawn.
Ever fleeting, ever near,
Chasing shadows without fear.

In pursuit of dusk's soft curtain,
Questions rise yet answers certain.
Mysteries of night unfold,
As shadows' tales are softly told.

## **Beneath the Surface**

Ripples dance on silent lakes,
Secrets lie where vision breaks.
Fragile mirrors 'neath the skin,
Veils of worlds that lie within.

Underneath the water's sheen,
Dreams obscure and thoughts serene.
Hidden depths where truths reside,
Life and love in shadows hide.

In the stillness, whispers call,
Buried echoes rise and fall.
Beneath the surface, time suspends,
Fathomed depths where journey ends.

Eyes that see beyond the veil,
Glimpse the heart where secrets sail.
Through the glassy, mirrored trace,
Reflections show a hidden face.

Down below where light is thin,
Worlds commence and dreams begin.
Beneath the surface, truths emerge,
In the quiet, shadows surge.

## **Shadow's Endgame**

In twilight's soft embrace
Where all shadows bend
A game of hide and seek begins
Till shadows find their end

In corners dark, they dwell
With whispers of the night
Unseen footprints leave their trail
In absence of the light

The sun will rise anew
Chasing darkness far
Shadows fade to morning hues
As day reclaims its star

But night will come again
With shadows to befriend
Their game eternal in its span
Till time sees their end

For every shadow cast
A dance with light ensues
In cycles ever vast
The shadows must pursue

**Translucent Allusions**

In mirrors we perceive
A realm of hazy forms
Where truths and lies interweave
In translucent norms

Reflections of the soul
In glassy, fragile panes
Whisper secrets never whole
In woven, clear refrains

Figures ghostlike stroll
Through corridors of mist
With dreams beyond control
In shadows that persist

Glimpses of what was
Or what could come to be
In the glass, we pause
To see our reality

Yet all remains unclear
In this translucent play
As past and future shear
The illusions of the day

## Masked Daydreams

Behind the fabric lies
A world of hidden dreams
Where fantasy complies
With all it truly seems

Masks upon our face
We wander through the haze
In a masquerade of grace
That colors all our days

Each mask a different shade
Of the selves we wish to be
In the grand parade
Of our masked reverie

To daydreams, we succumb
In this world of veiled deceit
Where masked desires hum
In rhythms bittersweet

Till the masks must fall
And truth will have its say
In the unmasked call
Of the light's pure, raw day

## **Wavering Realities**

In the space between breaths
Where realities waver
Time's soft tether frets
In dimensions we savor

Moments stretch and fray
Like spider silk in breeze
In surreal arrays
Of possible realities

Lines of fate entwine
In patterns undelineated
As cosmic hands design
Worlds ever animated

Waves of chance collide
Creating worlds a-new
As uncertainty abides
In every shifting view

Realities may blend
In a dance of twilight's grace
Where endings sweetly bend
To beginnings' warm embrace

## **Deceptive Horizons**

Beyond the fading twilight's gleam,
A world unseen, a distant dream,
Whispers dance on edge of sight,
In shadows cast by waning light.

Mirages paint the skies with hue,
Promises veiled in misty blue,
Step by step, the path misleads,
As truth and fiction interweave.

Chasing suns that never set,
Longing hearts with hope beset,
The farther reached, the less we see,
A sea of doubt, a windswept plea.

In the dusk of certainty,
Adventurers are set free,
For in the end, the voyage lies,
Beyond deceptive horizons' skies.

Hold fast to stars that bear no guise,
To navigate the night's disguise,
The journey's end, or so it seems,
Is found within our deepest dreams.

## Gossamer Lies

Silken threads of half-heard truths,
Weave their way through hearts of youth,
Gossamer lies in twilight spun,
Twist and twine till day is done.

In the whispers of the breeze,
Secrets hum through ancient trees,
Promises like morning dew,
Evaporate in sun's first view.

Facades shimmer, masks held high,
Truth obscured in evening sky,
Fingers grasp at shadows thin,
Lost in webs we wander in.

Through the haze of soft deceit,
Tread with caution, agile feet,
For every word, a silver strand,
Delicate in trembling hand.

Eyes that seek with earnest plea,
On the edge of mystery,
Shine the light through veils untrue,
Pierce the heart of gossamer blue.

## Shimmering Phantoms

Glint of light on edge of gloom,
Whispers from an empty room,
Figures dance in shadows brief,
Fading quick like autumn leaf.

In the twilight's fleeting glow,
Shimmers, flickers come and go,
Phantoms draped in silver night,
Caught between the day and night.

Voices echo soft and thin,
Laughter borne on zephyr's whim,
Reach to touch what isn't there,
Naught but glimmers in the air.

Glimpses of what might have been,
Dreams that flit on unseen wind,
Ephemeral as morning mist,
Moments lost, yet still persist.

Through the corridors of time,
Haunt the shadows, softly chime,
Shimmering phantoms, are you real?
Or just visions, thoughts conceal?

## Phantasmagoria

Realm of dreams both grand and stark,
Canvas painted after dark,
Twisted forms and colors bright,
Dance beneath the moon's cold light.

Surreal shadows, restless sweep,
Through the halls where secrets keep,
Mirrored halls of endless twist,
Lost in realms of fleeting mist.

Figures ghostly, faceless prance,
In an otherworldly trance,
Phantoms conjured from the mind,
In these maze-like visions bind.

Ephemeral the sights that pass,
Through the rippling looking glass,
Time and space, in fragments scored,
In phantasmagoric hoard.

In this carnival bizarre,
Truth and dream lie not afar,
Phantasmagoria does weave,
Spellbound tales, in webs that cleave.

## Ephemeral Mirrors

In fleeting glass reflections dance,
Moments shift in transient trance,
Figures waver, thoughts dissolve,
Mirrored worlds that all revolve.

Whispers echo, spoken past,
Shadows morph, but never last,
Each glance caught in liquid light,
Disappears with coming night.

Phantoms call from depths unknown,
Fleeting glimpses overthrown,
In the ripples, truths reside,
Fleeting, gone, but amplified.

## **Fogbound Realities**

Shrouded lands in misty grace,
Veiled and hidden, altering pace,
Steps unsure on pathways dim,
Bound by fog, reality thin.

Figures drift in hazy scenes,
Clinging close to phantom dreams,
Lines between the real and not,
Blended in this foggy plot.

Beyond, a world remains unclear,
Truths obscured by drifting sheer,
In this realm where mind concedes,
Fogbound worlds plant cryptic seeds.

## **Subtle Veils**

Gentle whispers softly blend,
Filters of a view pretend,
Layers thin yet strong they hold,
Stories wrapped in threads of gold.

Hidden meanings, cloaked intent,
In each veil a secret sent,
Through the woven, silent ties,
Seek the truth behind disguise.

Curtains drawn with sheer delight,
Unveil facets of the night,
Within veils, the heart's desire,
Flickers like a distant fire.

## Chasing Ephemera

Fleeting moments catch the wind,
Tiny sparks of dreams rescind,
Chasing shadows, wisps of flame,
Ephemera without name.

Glimmers there, and gone so swift,
Elusive as the morning drift,
In their trace, a hint remains,
Fleeting yet, what worth contains.

Bound by longing, spirits chase,
Each ethereal, fleeting grace,
Through the ephemeral mist we stride,
Dreams but danced, and seldom tied.

## The Dance of the Elusive

A shadow slips through moonlit beams,
A figure lost in whispered dreams,
It twirls and fades from sight unseen,
A phantom swirls in midnight's gleam.

Steps soft as whispers on the breeze,
A dance that never seems to cease,
Elusive as the fleeting seas,
It moves with silent, ghostly ease.

In twilight's arms it finds its grace,
A waltz that time cannot erase,
A fleeting glimpse, a hidden trace,
The dance it leaves to none replace.

Through starlit realms it winds and twists,
A ballet shrouded in the mists,
Ethereal and unconfined,
The dance remains undefined.

The night will end, the dawn will break,
But still the echoes it will make,
A memory that none can stake,
Of the dance that none could fake.

## **Mirrors in the Mist**

Reflections lost in morning's dew,
Where ghosts of yesterdays come through,
The mirror's mist obscures the view,
Of past and future, old and new.

Through cloudy glass the images play,
Echoes of what once was stay,
In misty veils, where shadows lay,
Mirrors in the mist display.

Fragments of time in silvered hues,
Memories obscured, confusing clues,
Fleeting faces, faintly fused,
In mercurial mist, diffused.

Shapes and forms from realms unknown,
In the mist, realities are shown,
Visions that the fog has sewn,
Unclaimed stories, seeds not sown.

The mist may rise, the vision part,
Yet in the soul, it leaves a start,
A haunting whisper in the heart,
Of mirrors in the mist, an art.

## **Fading Echoes**

The whispers of the past recede,
In shadows where the memories bleed,
Faint echoes lost in time's own speed,
The fading of an ancient creed.

Voices once strong, now drift away,
In twilight's dance, they softly sway,
Like autumn leaves on a breezy day,
Their presence begins to fray.

A melody that once was clear,
Floats on, but no one hears,
A song that slowly disappears,
Drowned by the flood of years.

Footsteps fade on paths once known,
A ghostly trail where life has flown,
In empty halls, their essence shown,
In silence, they stand alone.

The echoes faint, but not quite gone,
They dim but still, they linger on,
In hearts, their remnants now drawn,
Fading echoes at the break of dawn.

## **Shifting Realities**

In realms where dreams and waking blend,
The lines of truth and fiction bend,
A world where shadows twist and fend,
In shifting realities, we ascend.

A place where solid ground gives way,
To drifting sands and sky of gray,
In twilight's realm, where dawn holds sway,
Reality begins to stray.

Faces morph with each new scene,
In landscapes that have never been,
Fantasy and fact convene,
In visions odd, yet so serene.

Time unwinds, and streams reverse,
An ever-changing universe,
In the mind, the verse disperses,
In shifting dreams, we immerse.

Awake, asleep, the border thins,
As the dance of change begins,
A world where loss and finding wins,
In shifting realms where truth spins.

## Whispered Reflections

In shadows deep, where silence clings,
Soft whispers weave through moonlight's beams,
Echoes of dreams on silver wings,
Dance through the night like fleeting streams.

A murmur here, a sighing there,
Reflections drift on water's face,
Fading whispers fill the air,
In moonlit glades, lost time's embrace.

Silent voices from the past,
Their memories in twilight's sweep,
Through mirrored lakes, they wander fast,
In whispered vows, their secrets keep.

**Ghostly Horizons**

Beyond the veil where shadows roam,
The ghostly horizon softly glows,
A spectral light in twilight's dome,
Where time's forgotten river flows.

Ethereal forms in mist appear,
Dancing on the edge of night,
They whisper truths we long to hear,
In haunting tones, both faint and bright.

Celestial paths through endless skies,
Lead wandering souls to realms unseen,
Ghostly horizons softly sigh,
With memories of what has been.

## Labyrinth of Smoke

In curling plumes that rise and drift,
A labyrinth of smoke unfurls,
Through shifting haze, our thoughts uplift,
In spirals, secrets softly swirl.

Veiled passages, obscured and dim,
Winding trails of ashen grey,
Through shifting paths our fates begin,
In smoke's embrace, we lose our way.

In tendrils' dance, the past entwines,
Its shadows whisper in the dark,
Navigating smoke's thin lines,
We search for light, a distant spark.

## **Hollow Specters**

In ancient halls where echoes sleep,
Hollow specters softly tread,
Through corridors where shadows creep,
Their silent whispers fill with dread.

On haunted winds, their tales resound,
Of long-lost times, of grief, of woe,
In silent cries, their voices found,
A mournful dirge from long ago.

Through empty rooms, their steps do trace,
A ghostly dance of sorrow's plight,
In hollow eyes, the night's embrace,
In spectral form, they flee the light.

## Paradoxical Dreams

In slumber's realm, where thoughts do weave,
A tapestry of what to believe.
Contradictions blend, hopes intertwine,
In paradoxical dreams, so divine.

A silent scream, a joyful tear,
Confounding all that we hold dear.
Lost in mazes, yet roads are clear,
In mind's realm where none adhere.

Mountains float and rivers stay,
Stars dance in the light of day.
Truth and fiction mold like clay,
In dreams, where none can betray.

Ephemeral yet deeply real,
Shadows touch, and whispers feel.
Questions answered yet concealed,
Reality's edge softly peeled.

From chaos blooms the quiet peace,
All constraints begin to cease.
Paradoxical dreams never release,
Hearts in harmony, finding ease.

## Fleeting Phantasms

Whispers heard in twilight's glow,
Shapes that flit, yet do not show.
Moments lost, as breezes blow,
Fleeting phantasms come and go.

Specters vanish in the dawn,
Dreams forgotten, yet still drawn.
Faces fade as night withdraws,
Leaving echoes of what was.

Colors blend in spectral hues,
Chasing shadows, we confuse.
Mystic scenes in mind's own muse,
Reality's thin, fragile ruse.

Ethers blend and time does skew,
Reality splits into two.
So grasp these wisps of morning dew,
For phantasms will bid adieu.

Through the veil of dreams they play,
Dancing till the break of day.
In our hearts they softly stay,
Fleeting phantasms lead the way.

**Elusive Echoes**

In the stillness, faintly heard,
Are the whispers of a word.
Stories breathe without a sound,
Elusive echoes all around.

Shadows cast by moments gone,
Words once spoken, now withdrawn.
In the silence they prolong,
Ghostly whispers of a song.

Memories that slip through grasp,
In the quiet, voices rasp.
Through the ages, shadows clasp,
Elusive echoes, they enclasp.

Time's illusions, gently wave,
Through the corridors they pave.
Echoes linger, bold yet brave,
In silence, they softly stave.

Lost to time, yet not erased,
In our hearts, a spectral trace.
Elusive echoes interlace,
In the quiet, we embrace.

## Unseen Puppeteer

Behind the curtain, strings unseen,
Guiding moves, a hidden sheen.
Life and love in puppet's dance,
Woven through by unseen chance.

Hands that mold the fate of all,
Silent whispers rise and fall.
Threads of destiny in thrall,
Unseen puppeteer's soft call.

In the shadows, deftly play,
Weaving night into the day.
Silent force in grand array,
Guiding hearts in subtle sway.

Masks that hide the guiding hand,
Movements crafted, planned or bland.
Invisible, yet firm they stand,
Puppeteer's silent command.

Yet in the dance, we find our way,
Through the night and in the day.
Unseen force, we might obey,
To live and love, come what may.

## Spectral Tapestries

In twilight's weave, where shadows play,
The spectral tapestries display.
Ghostly threads in moonlit hue,
Whisper secrets old, anew.

Through mist they dance, in silent grace,
Ethereal forms with pale embrace.
Their stories linger, draped in air,
Lost in webs of time's own care.

Each shimmered strand, a past's delight,
Woven tight in phantom light.
So soft they touch, so light they bind,
The echoes of a world left behind.

Isolated, yet intertwined,
These spirits of the dream unkind.
Yet in their tapestry made of night,
They find solace, fleeting bright.

In shadows deep, their worlds collide,
Spectral tapestries never tied.
Unravelled dreams in silver spun,
Whispered tales of what's begun.

## Whims of Light

In dawn's soft bloom, where sunbeams play,
The whims of light come out to stay.
They frolic 'cross the morning dew,
And paint the skies in pastel hue.

They dance upon each blade and leaf,
In fleeting moments, bright yet brief.
A symphony of purest gold,
In nature's arms, a story told.

Through windows touched by morning's kiss,
They weave their magic, endless bliss.
Caressing shapes with tender might,
These whims of light, so pure, so bright.

They waltz within the softest breeze,
And pierce the canopy of trees.
In prismic flights of joy and glee,
They set our hearts and spirits free.

As day unfolds, their dance persists,
With mystic grace, they still exist.
A fleeting glimpse of day's pure art,
The whims of light, they touch the heart.

## Phantasmal Paths

On phantasmal paths where shadows tread,
Between the waking and the dead.
Whispered footsteps on the breeze,
Veiled in dark, beneath the trees.

Their silent steps on ether's thread,
Lead the way where dreams have bled.
A path unseen, yet deeply known,
In realms of moonlit, mystic tone.

Through corridors of mist they glide,
With no true end, no certain side.
Each step a whisper, soft, surreal,
With every stride, a vision's seal.

In twilight's hush, they lose their shade,
On paths where ghostly memories fade.
Yet mark their way with spectral sign,
Guiding souls to realms divine.

These phantasmal paths, ethereal, fair,
Lead to realms both rich and rare.
In hushed embrace of shadowed light,
They disappear into the night.

## Crystal Ghosts

Upon the dawn of snow and frost,
Where winter's breath is never lost.
There dwell unseen, in glacial hosts,
The fragile forms of crystal ghosts.

They shimmer in the morning's glare,
Ethereal in the frigid air.
Their icy breaths a haunting song,
In shadows, where the nights are long.

They wander through the frozen glades,
In icy silence, cool cascades.
With whispers cold, they weave their tales,
Through wintry winds and frosted veils.

These ghosts of crystal's sharp design,
Hold memories in cold confines.
Each flake a world, a dream entombed,
In winter's heart, where silence bloomed.

Yet as the sun begins to rise,
They fade away from waking eyes.
The crystal ghosts in cold repose,
Dissolve into the morning's glow.

## Gossamer Realities

In the twilight, dreams unfold,
Gossamer threads weave untold,
Whispers of what could be,
Dance in air, wild and free.

Forgotten hopes, soft and bright,
Hover there in fading light,
Illusions of realms afar,
Shimmer as a distant star.

Transient shapes in moonlit haze,
Mysteries in a quiet gaze,
Reality and dreams entwine,
In a moment so divine.

Fragile as a spider's silk,
Draped in hues of twilight's milk,
Ephemeral, the visions flee,
Into the night, silently.

And as the morning sun appears,
Dispelling all our twilight fears,
Gossamer dreams retreat away,
Awaiting the return of day.

## Hallucinated Paths

Walking down these winding ways,
Mirrored dreams obscure the days,
Echoes of a hidden truth,
Whisper in the careless youth.

Veins of light in shadows traced,
Wanderers in dreams embraced,
Serpentine, the pathways twist,
Through the fog and silver mist.

Every step a fleeting glance,
At fantasies that waltz and prance,
Reality, a fragile thread,
Among the visions in my head.

Labyrinths of star-lit lands,
Glimpse the touch of ghostly hands,
Guiding us through realms unseen,
On the edge of what has been.

As the dawn breaks through the night,
Scattering dreams with morning light,
Hallucinated paths dissolve,
New realities evolve.

## **Fleeting Shadows**

Beneath the crest of twilight's veil,
Fleeting shadows softly sail,
Through the garden of the night,
Fading fast at morning's light.

Figures move in silent grace,
Dancing through the evening's lace,
Momentary shades arise,
To disappear before our eyes.

Mystic echoes in the gloom,
Whisper tales of secret rooms,
Veiling truths in darkened folds,
Secrets by the night patrols.

Dew-kissed dreams in shadows twine,
Evanescent, they align,
Shifting with the lunar beams,
Ever caught in twilight's schemes.

With the dawn, they lose their reign,
Flee through sunlight's golden plane,
Fleeting shadows, once were near,
Diffused by day, they disappear.

## **Dim Entanglements**

In the web of night, we lie,
Dim entanglements of sky,
Threads of darkness twist and curl,
In a silent, midnight whirl.

Woven tales of dreams and fears,
Spun with silver, wet with tears,
Etched in starlight's tender glow,
In a dance both soft and slow.

Lost within this shadowed loom,
Hidden truths obscure the gloom,
Echoes of what once was clear,
Muffled now by twilight's ear.

Interlaced with darker strands,
Guided by unseen hands,
Fate and choice swirled in a sphere,
Binding all we hold dear.

As the dawn begins to break,
Threads of night begin to shake,
Dim entanglements unwind,
Leaving daylight intertwined.

## The Mirage Waltz

In twilight's gentle, shifting dance,
Shadows and light in wild romance,
A fleeting glimpse, a secret glance,
The horizon's line, a whispered trance.

Desert winds, a lonesome hum,
Echoes of what is yet to come,
Phantom steps to a silent drum,
Where dreams and reality succumb.

Sand and sky in fleeting flare,
Whispers float on arid air,
Illusions waltz with tender care,
A dance of visions rare and rare.

Mirage of water, cool embrace,
Chasing shadows in hidden place,
Yearning for the ghostly grace,
A timeless waltz we long to chase.

Through endless dunes, the rhythm plays,
A dance of light in golden haze,
Mirage waltz, ephemeral phase,
Slips through the night, fades with the days.

## Refraction of Truth

In prisms bright, the truth refracts,
Where shadows whisper, light reacts,
An arc of colors, facts abstract,
In bending light, reality contracts.

Through crystal glass, the world distils,
Fragments of truth in scattered quills,
Broken mirrors, silent thrills,
The essence of existence spills.

A ray, a beam, a fractured line,
Contours shifting, undefined,
In luminescent strands we find,
The truth within, unmet, confined.

Spectrum's dance, a fleeting glance,
Seeking balance in the chance,
A mosaic of what lies askance,
Unveiling truths in circumstance.

Refracted light, a tale reveals,
Of hidden depths and secret seals,
In vibrant hues, the truth conceals,
A mirrored world, where spirit heals.

## Hallucination Tides

In the sea of dreams, the wave forms rise,
Mirrors of madness in the skies,
Fleeting, shifting, in disguise,
The tides of mind with lunar ties.

Phantom ships on spectral seas,
Sailing through eternity's breeze,
Reality bends with eerie ease,
In hallucinations, peace deceives.

Whispers of the ocean's call,
Echoes in the twilight sprawl,
Waves of visions, rise and fall,
In the silent depths, we are enthralled.

Boundless tides in endless flow,
A dance of shadows in moon's glow,
Hallucinations come and go,
In the tides, the lines below.

In the ebb and flow, truths unveil,
In whispered tones, they softly hail,
Through hallucinations, we set sail,
In tides of dreams, we shall prevail.

## The Masked Canvas

On the canvas stretched and white,
Colors blend in shadowed light,
Masks we wear in day and night,
In painted realms, we take our flight.

Brushstrokes of a hidden face,
Conceal the truths we dare not trace,
In layers thick, with muted grace,
A masquerade in art's embrace.

Silent hues and muted tones,
Speak of stories, whispered moans,
Unveiling secrets, time condones,
Through painted lies, the truth atones.

In palettes rich, the masks align,
Truth and fiction intertwine,
In every stroke, a crafted sign,
On the masked canvas, we define.

A world concealed within the frame,
Where nothing stays, yet all proclaim,
In art's embrace, we stake our claim,
Behind the masks, we're all the same.

## Woven Shades

Through twilight's gauzy, woven shades,
Where secrets whisper in the glades,
Mysterious, the night invades,
While dreams in shadowed echoes fade.

A dance of dusk in silent grays,
As streaks of moonlight softly blaze,
Across the hills and empty bays,
Where tangled thoughts like rivers maze.

In quiet nooks where phantoms stroll,
Their whispers brush against the soul,
We weave our fears into a whole,
And let the silent darkness roll.

The woven shades, a silent vow,
Hold mysteries we disavow,
Yet in the dark, we find somehow,
The fears that yesterday did plow.

## **Veiled Chimeras**

Veiled chimeras drift through dreams,
Ephemeral as morning beams,
Their silence hides in whispered seams,
And masks the truth beneath its schemes.

In misty realms where phantoms glide,
Where hopes and fears slowly collide,
We chase the shadows that abide,
Yet grasp but echoes that divide.

These spectral forms, they come and go,
With eyes that glimmer, faintly glow,
They murmur secrets none shall know,
And leave us questioning the show.

Through veils, our senses oft deceive,
Chimeras make us dare believe,
In wonders we cannot perceive,
Then vanish with the light of eve.

## Elusive Echoes

Elusive echoes softly play,
In haunted hearts they find their stay,
Refrains of moments gone astray,
Ghostly whispers in the gray.

These echoes from the past arise,
To stir the dreams that once held skies,
They drift through nights with silent sighs,
Recalling truths wrapped in disguise.

In quiet corners, shadows cast,
Reflections of a distant past,
Whispers of what could not last,
And fragments of our memories vast.

Through halls of time their voices call,
We strain to hear the faintest thrall,
But echoes fade, resist our thrall,
And leave us grasping as they fall.

## **Shimmering Haze**

Beneath a sky of shimmering haze,
Where sunlight swirls in golden phase,
The world becomes a soft malaise,
A dreamy dance in summer's gaze.

The horizon blurs in distance keen,
With hues of violet, soft and green,
A painter's touch on nature's screen,
In scenes both vibrant and serene.

The air is laden with the scent,
Of blooming fields and days well-spent,
In whispered breezes heaven-sent,
We find a peace with pure intent.

The shimmering haze, it wraps us tight,
In beauty's glow, in vibrant light,
Transforming day to gentle night,
And dreams to sparkles in our sight.

## **Enigmatic Hues**

In twilight's grasp the colors blend,
Mysterious and deep they wend,
Through shadows thick, through twilight's lens,
Their secrets lost, they twist and bend.

A swirling mist of blue and green,
Bright crimson threads and gold unseen,
They whisper tales to those who dream,
Of worlds unknown, a distant gleam.

Silent winds weave stories old,
In enigmatic hues enfold,
A tapestry of myths retold,
In twilight's arms, a sight to hold.

The night descends, its canvas drawn,
With shades of dusk till breaking dawn,
These cryptic hues, they come, they're gone,
A fleeting glimpse, a cosmic yawn.

In twilight's grip, a riddle framed,
Of colors wild and untamed,
An endless dance, forever named,
Enigmatic hues, enthralled, unclaimed.

## **Paradox of Light**

In beams of light that pierce the dark,
A paradox ignites a spark,
Where shadows meld with blinding bright,
A dance emerges, day and night.

With photons clashing in their flight,
Creating realms of fleeting sight,
The seamless blend of black and white,
A paradox, they both unite.

In twilight's realm where contrasts meet,
A cosmic truth, a truth discreet,
Where dark and light in tandem beat,
An endless cycle, pure, complete.

Reflections cast on rippling streams,
Illuminate our waking dreams,
In paradox, the harmony seems,
A woven fabric, truth redeems.

Amidst the glow, the shade consumes,
A paradox of twilit rooms,
In every spark, a shadow blooms,
In light's embrace, the dark resumes.

## Celestial Wraiths

In boundless skies where stars ignite,
Celestial wraiths traverse the night,
Their ghostly forms in silent flight,
Eternal roamers, spirits bright.

Through cosmic seas they softly glide,
On argent winds they gently ride,
Across the void, where dreams reside,
Their whispered songs, the heavens guide.

In nebulous mists, they weave their tale,
Where time stands still, and echoes pale,
They chart the course, where hopes prevail,
In stardust paths, their wings unveil.

Amidst the stars, in twilight's grasp,
Celestial wraiths in silence clasp,
The fleeting moments they enwrap,
In cosmic dance, their secrets rasp.

In realms unseen, where starlight fades,
They wander through the endless shades,
Eternal wraiths, whose light pervades,
In cosmic spheres, their legacy wades.

## **Fading Facades**

In shadows long, where echoes play,
The fading facades in disarray,
Their whispered tales of yesterday,
Erode with time, and drift away.

Through halls of time, the faces pass,
Reflections caught in panes of glass,
Forgotten dreams in tarnished brass,
Their essence fades, a fleeting mass.

With every dawn, a mask is shed,
The colors bleed, the lines are spread,
A story old, a path retread,
In twilight's glow, the past is read.

In whispered winds of dusk's descent,
The fading facades are gently sent,
Through veils of time, the night invents,
A shifting dance, a truth lament.

The echoes fade, the colors blur,
A tapestry of things that were,
In twilight's grasp, they softly purr,
Fading facades, their whispers stir.

## Mirage of Mind

In the desert of thoughts, a mirage gleams,
Fleeting and fickle, like distant dreams.
Oasis of wisdom, just beyond reach,
A silent lesson it wishes to teach.

Mind wanders through sands, seeking truth,
Footsteps erase the knowledge of youth.
Mirage dissolves in the light of day,
Yet shadows of doubt ever linger and sway.

Illusions dance on the horizon line,
Minds thirst for answers, perception's wine.
Ephemeral wisdom slips through the hand,
As we traverse this thought-filled land.

Hope rises like the morning sun,
But doubts linger when day is done.
Mirages fade but the quest remains,
In the fertile soil of searching brains.

Thoughts converge like desert winds,
Whispering secrets, bearing sins.
Mirage of mind, keepers of keys,
To unlock the mysteries of you and me.

## Whispers of the Veil

Beneath the moon's soft, silvered glow,
Veils of night conceal what we know.
Whispers travel on the evening breeze,
Ghostly secrets rustle through the trees.

In twilight's arms, the world is hushed,
Veiled voices of the past are flushed.
From shadows deep, murmurs arise,
Telling tales under starlit skies.

Eyes closed tight, the veil unfurls,
Revealing wonders and hidden pearls.
Dreams and memories softly blend,
Where whispers of the veil ascend.

Night's cloak wraps around the land,
In silent language we understand.
The veil is thin, the whispers clear,
Revealing truths we hold so dear.

At dawn's break, the whispers fade,
Daylight pierces the night's charade.
Yet echoes of the veil remain,
In hearts that remember the night's refrain.

## Shattered Reflections

In the mirror's silvered gleam,
We see the fragments of a dream.
Shattered reflections, truth unveiled,
Scattered pieces, stories regaled.

Broken glass, each shard a tale,
Fractured moments that prevail.
We pick them up, one by one,
Under the light of a dying sun.

In each splinter, a piece of soul,
We search for parts to make us whole.
Shattered reflections, mosaic bright,
Piecing together the dark and light.

Through cracks and fissures, light seeps in,
Illuminating where we have been.
Each reflection a lesson learned,
In the vase of life, we're gently turned.

Mirror mends with patient hands,
Understanding what it demands.
Shattered reflections, a canvas clear,
True beauty found in what's sincere.

**Dreams of Smoke**

In twilight hours, dreams arise,
Soft smoke dances, clouds disguise.
Ephemeral whispers, barely spoke,
Are woven in the dreams of smoke.

Eyes closed tight, the visions swirl,
Like mist that in the night unfurls.
Dreams of smoke, elusive and fleet,
Vanishing like the morning sleet.

Within the haze, hopes ignite,
Fleeting glimpses of distant light.
Dreams of smoke, forever swaying,
In the realm where night is laying.

Through the fog, desires form,
Tracing patterns with ghostly warm.
In ethereal webs, futures cloak,
Woven tight in dreams of smoke.

As dawn approaches, dreams recede,
Fading gently as the hour decreed.
But memories linger, softly awoke,
From the whispers in dreams of smoke.

## Tales in Vapor

Whispers ride on misty threads,
Stories told where shadows spread.
Ink dissolves in morning dew,
Words, like ghosts, elusive too.

Beneath the fog, the past is veiled,
Secrets in the silence hailed.
Ancient echoes softly play,
Vapor guides the lost away.

Gentle tendrils twist and twine,
Spoken thoughts in rhythm chime.
Memories dissolve in breeze,
Truths concealed in mysteries.

Breath of fog, a fleeting sight,
Ancient tales in transient light.
Dreams that form and drift afar,
Shrouded in a spectral star.

Ethereal paths we tread alone,
In the vapor, tales are sown.
Silent voices, whispered lore,
Boundless seas of mist explore.

## Soft Eclipses

Moonlight dances on the brink,
Stars in shadow slowly sink.
Celestial whispers fill the air,
Soft eclipses, moments rare.

Nighttime's curtain gently falls,
Darkness wraps the world in thralls.
Silken shadows weave a song,
Through the stillness, echoes long.

Glimmers fade in twilight's clasp,
Holding fast to night's last gasp.
In the hush, a secret blooms,
Soft eclipses, subtle tunes.

Luminous trails wane and grow,
In the twilight's gentle flow.
Silent peace in night's embrace,
Soft eclipses, time and space.

Dreams unfold in muted hue,
Midnight whispers, softly true.
Through the darkened skies they creep,
Soft eclipses, calming sleep.

## Evaporated Gleams

Morning breaks in silver light,
Shimmering, dissolving night.
Gleams evaporate in air,
Casting whispers, soft and rare.

Sunrise paints the sky with fire,
Moments fleeting, brief desire.
Golden threads in dawn's embrace,
Evaporated gleams, a trace.

Memories alight then fade,
In the morning's bright parade.
Dewdrops shimmer, then they part,
Fleeting gleams, the day's new start.

On the breeze, the past dissolves,
Fractured light in orbits revolve.
Ephemeral, the morning beams,
Lost in mists, evaporated gleams.

Waking hours bloom then pass,
Moments shatter like the glass.
Daylight wanes, the cycle leans,
Into dusk, evaporated gleams.

## **Drifting Specters**

In the pale of midnight's glow,
Drifting specters come and go.
Ethereal shapes that pass unseen,
Through the realms of in-between.

Whispers stir the autumn leaves,
Carried on the ghostly breeze.
Phantoms tread where shadows lie,
Silent paths where echoes die.

Moonlight casts a silver veil,
Drifting specters gently sail.
Haunting dreams in night's domain,
Fleeting shadows, soft refrain.

Spectral forms in twilight's keep,
Voices lost in silent weep.
Through the darkness, they disperse,
Drifting specters, whispered verse.

Dawn approaches, shadows flee,
Drifting specters cease to be.
In the light, their secrets hide,
Morning sun their fates decide.

## Fanciful Phantoms

In twilight's gentle, quiet reign,
Phantoms dance through misty lane,
Forgotten dreams, a spectral flight,
Whispered tales in moon's soft light.

They float above the earthly ground,
With silent steps, they make no sound,
Echoes of the times once known,
A world of shadows, lost and grown.

The air is filled with ancient sighs,
Beneath the starlit, endless skies,
Their secret stories, thin as air,
Are carried by the night's cool stare.

Of joys and sorrows, deep and bright,
They weave their tale in silver light,
A fleeting glimpse, then gone once more,
In shadows past the forest floor.

## **Spectral Whispers**

Through the midnight's veiled embrace,
Whispers drift from time and place,
Ghostly voices softly call,
From the shadows, down the hall.

Glimpses of forgotten lore,
From days and nights that are no more,
Their secrets hid from mortal eyes,
In murmured tones, they softly rise.

Faint and fragile, on the breeze,
Stories carried with such ease,
Long-lost echoes, spectral song,
In the silence, they belong.

In the heart of night they roam,
Far from light and hearth and home,
Ever wandering, never still,
Silent guardians of the chill.

## Invisible Curves

Through the air, unseen they move,
Curves of whispers, shadows prove,
In the realm of hidden grace,
Faintest lines in secret space.

Silent sweep of unseen arcs,
Painting night with hidden marks,
Soft caress of phantom touch,
Shapes that linger, never much.

Bending light and bending time,
Through the spaces, they will climb,
Invisible to earthly gaze,
Tracing paths in starlit haze.

Patterns woven out of sight,
Curves that dance with dreamlike might,
In the night, the unseen play,
In their dance, they softly sway.

**Mirror's Ghost**

Gaze into the polished glass,
See reflections as they pass,
In the mirror, shadows play,
Ghosts of light and dark array.

Echoes of another realm,
Silent phantoms at the helm,
Twist and turn in mirrored sheen,
Figures lost in silvered screen.

Through the looking glass they glide,
In and out of mirrored tide,
Wending paths through shadow's seam,
Part of night and part of dream.

In the depths, a fleeting face,
Vanishes without a trace,
Ghostly whispers softly rise,
In the mirror's hidden guise.

## Crystal Phantasms

Gleaming shards in twilight's dance,
Fractured light through troubled glance,
Phantasms whisper, softly sing,
Wings of glass take shimmering swing.

Ethereal kingdoms rise and fall,
Echoing through nightly call,
Silent voices speak so clear,
Past and future drawing near.

Gossamer dreams in beauty's hand,
Crafted by a spectral band,
Crystalline journeys, wild and free,
Across the void, a starry sea.

Hallowed moments, frozen time,
Mystic rhythms, whispered rhyme,
In glittering flight, carry me,
Through realms of pure serenity.

Whispers fade in morning's light,
Ephemeral ghosts in fading night,
Crystal phantasms, tales untold,
Melt away, to light enfold.

**Vaporous Layers**

Waves of mist in morning's dawn,
Silent veils upon the lawn,
Layered whispers, soft and thin,
Guiding where the dreams begin.

Silver fog in folds embrace,
Every form and every space,
Vaporous layers, calmly flow,
Through the world we think we know.

Mystic currents, flowing light,
Stories woven from the night,
Ghostly shrouds in shadowed way,
Herald the departing day.

Through the haze, a shadow's dance,
In this cryptic, hazy trance,
We drift in films of twilight's care,
Through liquid worlds beyond compare.

As the sun with warmth ignites,
Curtains drawn to daylight's rights,
Vaporous layers, thin to none,
And fade away with rising sun.

## **Shadows of Mirage**

Under sun in desert's gold,
Mirage of tales yet to be told,
Shadows flicker, dance and sway,
Glory of a phantom's day.

Rippling heat and wavy lines,
Mirrored lakes and phantom pines,
Ghostly ships on sandy seas,
Whisper secrets on the breeze.

In the mirage, a kingdom gleams,
Fleeting forms and quiet dreams,
Shadows cast by fevered mind,
Lost illusions of a kind.

Echoes of an ancient lore,
Seen but just, and nothing more,
Wandering eyes, a trickery,
In shadows of a mystery.

Dreams dissolve and shadows fall,
As night consumes us, one and all,
In Mirage's fleeting grace,
Only shadows leave a trace.

## Misted Reverie

In morning's hush, the mist appears,
Veils of time and shadowed years,
Soft and gentle, gray embrace,
Cradling secrets, lost of place.

Whispered words in vapor weave,
Thoughts and dreams in silence breathe,
Misted reverie, soft and slow,
Floating on the clouds below.

Ephemeral scenes in quiet's care,
Paintings formed by misty air,
Through this realm of tender gray,
Ghost-bound journeys find their way.

Soft as feathers, thoughts converge,
In this tranquil, muted surge,
Misted moments blend and twine,
In the depth of heart and mind.

When the sun emerges bright,
Dissolving mist in morning light,
Reveries of misted hue,
Depart, but leave a dream or two.

## **Hazy Realms**

In the haze where phantoms dwell,
Whispers weave their subtle spell,
Skies of twilight, dreams untold,
Mysteries in twilight's fold.

Shadows dance in lunar light,
Eclipsed in fog, and veiled in night,
Silhouettes of nonexistent things,
Flitting by on spectral wings.

Clocks that chime in silent tones,
Rivers flowing o'er forgotten stones,
Echoes of a distant shore,
Boundaries blurred forevermore.

Starry mist, horizon fades,
Secrets in the dusk parades,
Chasing whispers, night's embrace,
Hazy realms, a fleeting grace.

In a world of fleeting time,
Verse and riddle intertwine,
Hazy realms where dreams conspire,
Lighting hearts with spectral fire.

## Mirage Symphony

Mirage symphony, desert's song,
Notes that echo, wild and long,
Golden dunes that shift and sway,
Mirages at the break of day.

Winds compose a phantom choir,
Veils of sand that twirl and tire,
Patterns cast by sun's warm gleam,
Dancing through the daylight dream.

Silent whispers, secrets told,
In a symphony of old,
Echoes that the day revives,
In the sand's elusive lives.

Tempest strings and zephyr chimes,
Waltzing through the shifting times,
Barren waves that softly crest,
Harmony in earth's fine jest.

To the dune's ethereal spell,
Hearts are drawn, and minds compel,
Mirage symphony plays on,
Till the spectral notes are gone.

## **Fugitive Glimmers**

Fugitive glimmers, fleeting light,
Searching through the velvet night,
Stars that dart and swiftly fade,
Dreams within the shadows laid.

Glimpses of a hidden hue,
Moments gone before they're true,
Secrets in the night's embrace,
Lost within the endless chase.

Phantoms by the moon's soft gleam,
Fleeting whispers from a dream,
Fugitive in twilight's veil,
Glowing like a comet's trail.

Echoes of a silent plea,
Glimmers from a distant sea,
Emerald flares in sapphire skies,
Never caught by waking eyes.

Lingering, the glimpses break,
Memory of the lights they make,
Fugitive glimmers fade to dark,
Leaving but a fleeting spark.

## **Cloaked Mysteries**

Cloaked in whispers, night descends,
Mysteries that darkness sends,
Veiled pathways, shadows deep,
Secrets that the silence keep.

Midnight's breath, a soft caress,
Enigmas that the stars confess,
Shrouded tales in moonlight's glow,
Cloaked in mists of dreams below.

Eyes that glint in shadow's play,
Glimmers of a hidden way,
Threads of stories tightly spun,
Cloaked mysteries, never done.

Elusive specters in the mist,
Unknown shapes by twilight kissed,
Questions in the hush of night,
Seeking answers out of sight.

Wandering through the cloaked abyss,
Each enigma seals a kiss,
Nighttime's tapestry unfurls,
Cloaked mysteries in the world's.

## **The Vanishing Point**

Where the sky meets the sea, a line so thin,
Boundaries blur, reality wears thin.
Horizons whisper secrets, old and new,
Distance calls, and we bid adieu.

Footprints fade on the endless shore,
Time erases what came before.
Memories scatter like grains of sand,
Lost in the vastness, unplanned.

Ships set sail on a twilight quest,
Chasing a dream, yearning for rest.
Stars begin to shimmer in the night,
Guiding souls with ethereal light.

Mist rises from the ocean's breath,
Draping the world in a shroud of zest.
Ephemeral moments, fleeting, grand,
Transcend the mundane on this strand.

And as the sun dips low, then fades,
The vanishing point our spirit invades.
Light and shadow unite, converge,
In the twilight, we find our urge.

## Veil of Dreams

In twilight's gentle, silent embrace,
Dreams weave threads of hidden grace.
Stars peek through a translucent veil,
Whispering tales in the moonlit gale.

Soft murmurs of a phantom's song,
Echo in realms where dreams belong.
A dance of shadows, light, and shade,
Where waking moments softly fade.

Lanterns flicker in fantasy's mist,
Guiding travelers through night's twist.
Echoes of laughter, whispers of tears,
Blend in the silence, calm our fears.

Fields of wonder, scenes unfold,
More precious than the finest gold.
Bound by dreams, we journey far,
Navigating by an unseen star.

In the veil of dreams, the night does mend,
Wounds of the day as nighttime's friend.
We rise, we fall, we dream anew,
In ethereal realms, our spirits grew.

## **Veil of Whispers**

A veil of whispers, soft and low,
Carries secrets only night can know.
Mystic breezes dance with grace,
In the silence, whispers trace.

Leaves applaud the moon's ascent,
Nature's chorus, reverent.
Whispers float like gentle sighs,
Beneath the canopy of skies.

Echoes of a long-forgotten tale,
Drift on winds, so soft and frail.
Secrets shared, yet held so tight,
Under the stars, in tranquil night.

Veil of whispers, calm and clear,
Brings the distant ever near.
Words unspoken, truths revealed,
In the quiet night, gently sealed.

As dawn approaches, whispers fade,
Reality stirs, night's serenade.
But the veil remains, thin and bright,
Guarding whispers 'til the night.

## Mirage of Dreams

In desert sands, a vision blooms,
An oasis bathed in silver plumes.
Where reality and dreams entwine,
Mirage of dreams, a borderline.

Shimmering pools reflect the sky,
Illusions born where whirlwinds sigh.
Mirrors of hope in endless gold,
Stories of dreams, silently told.

Journeys taken on endless dunes,
Guided by ephemeral tunes.
Chasing shadows in light's embrace,
Dreams dissolve without a trace.

Palms sway in the mirage's hue,
Promising shade for the few.
An untouched realm, a fleeting sight,
Captures hearts in fragile light.

When sun dips low, the vision fades,
Mirage of dreams in twilight shades.
Yet in the heart, it lives and beams,
A sanctuary of distant dreams.

## **Echoes of the Disguised**

In shadows, whispers dance to none
Masks conceal the truth undone
Eyes behind a veil of night
Seek the voice, flee the light

Echoes mingle, softly speak
Truths, they fear, they never seek
Silent screams behind the guise
In the darkness, no surprise

Mirrors shatter, shards of lies
Reflect the past in dark disguise
Yet hope lingers in the glow
Of secrets that we dare not show

Underneath the silent sky
Lies the whisper of a sigh
Fear not the echo in the night
Embrace the dawn, embrace the light

Unveil the heart behind the quake
Let shadows fall, let voices quake
A truth concealed, a life disguised
In every echo, love survives.

## Façade of the Heart

Beneath the smile, a tear unseen
A story told in shades between
Eyes that sparkle, hearts concealed
Untold tales they dare not yield

The beating chest, a silent cry
In masquerades, the truths do lie
Each pulse a whisper of the art
Of secrets held within the heart

Masked emotions, fleeting glance
Every look a hidden dance
Yearning for a moment seen
To tear away what could have been

In the quiet, hearts do share
A secret longing, raw and bare
Shadows lift as light reveals
What every hidden heart conceals

Beyond the mask, a voice is heard
Softly spoken, every word
In love's tender, fragile part
Lies the true façade of the heart.

## **Masquerade of Time**

The clock ticks softly, hush to hear
A masquerade of time is near
Moments cloaked in veils of lace
Each second past, a hidden face

Through the dance, the hours glide
Masks of minutes never lied
A silent waltz, a secret rhyme
In the grand masquerade of time

Memories whisper, shadows blend
In the twirl, the past extend
The turn of ages, cycles spin
Reflected in the silent din

Moments slip through fingers' grasp
In every tick, a whispered gasp
Yet time's embrace, a gentle guide
In masks of night, we coincide

Each breath a step, each beat a sign
Draped in threads of grand design
Embrace the dance, in shadows prime
Join the masquerade of time.

## **Twilight Deceptions**

In the twilight, shadows play
Deceptions dance in the fading day
Light and dark a whispered blend
Truths unravel, lies contend

The dusk unfolds, a silent guise
Veils of silver mask the skies
Each star a secret, softly gleamed
Reflecting dreams we only dreamed

In twilight's breath, the heart's concealed
A mirrored glance of wounds unhealed
Yet in the dark, the truth remains
A whispered echo of our pains

Draped in twilight's tender shade
Dreams are born, and nightmares fade
A deception's silhouette appears
Entwined with love, entwined with fears

Seek the dawn, the break of light
Where shadows yield to morning's might
In the echoes of the night, confide
Embrace the twilight, never hide.

## **Echoes of a Phantom**

In the silence of the night, it calls
A whisper through the aged halls
Footsteps vanish, yet they seem
To haunt the remnants of a dream

Echoes of a phantom's tale
Through winds that wail, they sail
A shadow lost in moonlight's veil
With secrets only stars unveil

Memories in the corners creep
In darkness, they do softly seep
Hidden whispers, mysteries deep
In the silence, we find no sleep

A laughter faint, a lullaby
Ghostly sighs that drift and die
In twilight hues, they softly lie
Echoes of a phantom cry

Through realms unseen, they roam
In every creak, they find a home
In solitude, the phantoms roam
In echoes, they're forever known

## Shadows in the Mist

Beneath the veil of morning's shroud
Where silence reigns, no voices loud
Shadows drift like spirits proud
Softly through the mist, they're bowed

In twilight hours, secrets swirl
Whispers in the fog unfurl
Hidden paths in dreamy whirl
Through the mist, lost worlds unfurl

Phantoms in a gray disguise
Glide beneath the watchful skies
Their secrets shared in silent guise
Lost in depths where mystery lies

As dawn breaks through the hazy cloak
Shadows wane, though never broke
In mist, they linger, softly spoke
A hidden world, a secret token

Through valleys deep and forests wide
Where spectral beings choose to hide
In mist, the worlds of shadows bide
A realm where only dreams reside

## **Waves of Deception**

Upon the sea, a calm facade
Yet underneath, deceptions nod
Waves that churn with hidden plod
A dance concealed, a tangled fraud

Beneath the surface, currents twist
In shadows blue, they mesh and tryst
A truth obscured by ocean's mist
Betrayed by unseen, silent cyst

Tales of sailors lost in night
To waves that feign a tranquil sight
In their depths, a reckless flight
A struggle hidden from the light

Seas that whisper in deceit
Secrets held beneath the fleet
Waves that hide where truth and lie meet
A treacherous veil, a masked retreat

Navigating through the storm
In waters cold, the spirits warm
Waves of deception, eerily forlorn
In their depths, new realms are born